It's My Birthday

Written by Chemise Taylor

Illustrated by Alexis B. Taylor

Copyright © 2019 by My Skills Books

Published by My Skills Books

All rights reserved. No part of this publication may be reproduced, distributed, or transmitted in any form or by any means, including photocopying, recording, or other electronic or mechanical methods, without the prior written permission of the publisher, except in the case of brief quotations embodied in critical reviews and certain other noncommercial uses permitted by copyright law.

First Printing, 2019.

ISBN: 978-1-951573-02-7

www.myskillsbooks.com

Today is my birthday! I am turning one year older. I'm having a party and all of my friends are coming over.

I'm celebrating my birthday at my home.
We will dance and play games all day long.

We will eat pizza and cake. They are almost here. I can hardly wait!

Knock! Knock! Who do I see? All of my friends here to celebrate with me.

They sing, "Happy Birthday! You are smart, funny and kind. I'm happy I am your friend and you are mine."

I can't wait to open all of my gifts. But first let me blow out the candles and make a wish.

1....2...3....BLOW!

My friends say, "I wonder what he will wish for."

That is a secret, that I will not share.

I open my gifts. I got a ball, toy car and a big, brown bear.

Thank you, Lisa, Sharon, Amy and Gerald. You are the best friends in the world.

"This was so much fun. I'm glad you all were here."

"I'm excited for my birthday party, next year!"

Book Details

Story Word Count: 181

Key Words: Birthday, Party, Cake, Friends, Gifts, Year, Celebrate

Comprehension Check

- What was the story about?
- What gifts did he get?
- What were the names of his friends?

Reading Award

This certificate goes to:

_____

for reading "It's My Birthday"

Good Job!

More books, apps and resources at myskillsbooks.com

www.ingramcontent.com/pod-product-compliance
Lightning Source LLC
Chambersburg PA
CBHW042111090526

44592CB00004B/83